Radi os

Of Man's first disobedience, and the fruit
Of that forbidden **tree** whose mortal taste
Brought death **into the World,** and all our woe,
With loss of Eden, till one greater **Man**
Restore us, and regain the blissful seat,
Sing, Heavenly Muse, that, on the secret top
Of Oreb, or of Sinai, didst inspire
That shepherd who first taught **the chosen** seed
In the beginning how the heavens and earth
Rose out of Chaos: or, if Sion hill
Delight thee more, and Siloa's brook that flowed
Fast by the oracle of God, I thence
Invoke thy aid to my adventurous **song,**
That with no middle flight intends to soar
Above the Aonian mount, while it pursues
Things unattempted yet in prose or rhyme.

Ronald Johnson

Jaradis

Lost

FLOOD EDITIONS CHICAGO 2005

For permission, required to reprint or

broadcast more than several lines, write to:

FLOOD EDITIONS

Post Office Box 3865

Chicago, Illinois 60654-0865

www.floodeditions.com

ISBN 0-9746902-4-4

Designed by Quemadura

COVER ILLUSTRATIONS: Details from *Satan Watching
the Endearments of Adam and Eve* by William Blake,
courtesy of the Huntington Library, Art Collections,
and Botanical Gardens, San Marino, California

Printed in the United States of America

on acid-free, recycled paper

FIRST EDITION

The type stands as is: the "words" are those of an 1892 edition of *Paradise Lost* I picked off a Seattle bookshop shelf the day after hearing Lucas Foss' Baroque Variations. He writes of Variation I, on Handel's Concerto Grosso, Op. 6, No. 12, "Groups of instruments play the Larghetto but keep submerging into inaudibility (rather than pausing). Handel's notes are always present but often inaudible. The inaudible moments leave holes in Handel's music (I composed the holes). The perforated Handel is played by different groups of the orchestra in three different keys at one point, in four different speeds at another."

This is the first of three sections of four—Milton's divisions being twelve. It is the book Blake gave me (as Milton entered Blake's left foot—the first foot, that is, to exit Eden), his eyes wide open through my hand. *To etch* is "to cut away," and each page, as in Blake's concept of a book, is a single picture.

I would like particularly to thank Robert Duncan for his encouragement through my solitary quest in the cloud chamber—that place, he assured me, "The Authors are in Eternity."

Ronald Johnson

SAN FRANCISCO, 1976

radi os

O I

O
                        tree
                into the World,

                                    Man

                              the chosen

Rose out of Chaos:

                              song,

                              outspread,
                on the vast

Illumine,

I

  Say first—

                      what time

                              aspiring

                equal

Raise

          headlong

To bottomless
                              fire
          times the space that measures

                                        thought
Both
                                        eyes,

At once,

              on all sides round,

                                        fed
With
          place Eternal

In utter darkness,

     from the centre

                    whirlwind

     "If

Myriads

Joined
In Equal

               thunder:
The force of

                    outward lustre,   mind,

                         raised

Innumerable

                    on the plains of
And
All is
And
And
And
That

Who, from the terror of this

empyreal

Irreconcilable
of joy

answered

Too well I see

: for the mind

swallowed up

entire,

in the heart   to work in fire,

words the Arch

being

!

the gates of

lightning

through the vast and boundless

rest,

With head uplift above the wave, and eyes

Leviathan,

slumbering on the
small

tell,

rind,

the burning

dark designs,

How

wind transports a hill

conceiving fire,

Sublimed

the soil,

celestial

field

A mind   to be changed by place or
                              lace
                    Heaven of Hell,

                astonished on the oblivious pool,

                    the O

Of

        wonder,

                                        circumference
Hung on   shoulders like the moon, whose
            optic glass
At evening, from the top
                            new
                                    globe

Of some great

            burning
                    azure;
                            vaulted

Forms,
autumnal leaves
where

winds Orion

iris

wheels.

all the hollow deep

the Flow

To slumber
Or
adore
,
the flood

Transfix us
Awake,

Upon the wing, as

locusts, warping on the

numberless
under

upper, nether,

waving
balance
fill all the plain:

deluge

Forthwith, from every
head
—godlike Shapes, and Forms
cell

the invisible

by various name

on the bare

Between the

light.

man

passed through fire

His temple right against

The
    black

                 realm, beyond

The flower

who, from the bordering flood

Dilated or condensed,

    of love

            left

star

bright image

                            heart,

                           like heat

Ezekiel saw,
His eye

            against the

          Is

equal

To him no

                                        door
Exposed
                        the prime in order and in
        rest

                                                seized
By
                                measure found;

                        through all the bounds

                                        fields,
                                                Isles

In loss itself;

                        high words

Who

        meteor streaming to the wind,

      blowing

          concave, and beyond

   in a moment

Appeared,
Of depth immeasurable.
        phalanx
Of flutes and

                 pain

Breathing
      in silence

      they stand—
      and dazzling arms,

   number

    embodied

      —though all the giant

Mixed

And all

with all

above the rest

Stood
All

: as when the sun
Looks through the horizontal
behind the moon,
eclipse

Archangel:

heaven's fire

From wing to wing, and

Words interwove with
mortal
Matchless,

change
of mind,

For who can yet believe

                                        to re-ascend,
                and re-possess

                in close design,
At length from us

Space may produce new Worlds

                to pry

                                        Abyss

For who can think

                        the sudden blaze

There stood a hill

A numerous

              least erected

In vision

          the Centre,

             ribs of gold

                        and wondering

Of Babel,

               in many cells

                  of liquid fire

A various mould

                   the sound-board breathes.

            the earth a fabric

Built like a temple,   round

                        The ascending pile
Stood
Opening
Within,
And
Pendent by
        star

                    the crystal battlements:
                        from noon to

                    trumpet's sound,

And porches wide,

                        both on the ground and in the air,
                            As bees

                    the Sun
                                about the hive
        In clusters;
            to and fro

                    Earth's
                                arrow

            fountain,
            dream

                                            and dance

        At once
                        to smallest forms
                their shapes immense, and

                            far within,
                in their own dimensions

                                silence

radi os

o II

H^{igh}

Ind,

Beyond

imaginations

I
Celestial

: from this descent

next

Established in

                                        Thunderer's aim

                                        mind
To union,

              open

              with the Eternal

          sentence
                              :
                                        the rest—
The signal to ascend—

                        who

Turning
                        to meet the noise
                        shall hear
              and, for lightning, see

                              itself
                              strange fire,

              invented
The way seems difficult,
       upright   against
                         the sleepy drench
                           not still,
        our proper motion

           pursued
               and laborious
               ascent
The event

           unextinguishable
            without hope of end

Inexorably,

        substance

On this side nothing

        perpetual inroads

To less

the ear,

at our heels
With blackest
light,

ethereal mould,

:
to spend all

To perish

aware,

decreed,
to eternal
more,

What if the breath
Awaked, should
        plunge us into flames; or from above

                                        if all
            were opened,

One day upon our heads;

Each on his rock transfixed,

        all things at one view?

        then, live

                        at the spear

                in time

mind

changed at length,

the never-ending flight

with words

with what eyes could we

sing

By force impossible,

Live to ourselves, though in this vast recess,
to none

when great things of small,

We can create,

out of pain

Of darkness
an

unobscured
round

lustre

Become our element

,

All things

Compose
Of what we are and where,

the tempest

another field

within

and long process of time,

A pillar

               attention still as night

   we

                 build up
                    dream,

  This place
  Beyond

    highth or depth, still first and last

    sit we then projecting

     —another World,
       called Man

all our thought

                                              shut

utmost border
                  who hold it

headlong to

                        root,
To mingle and involve,

                    The bold design

           their eyes:

O   bright confines,

World?

the palpable

Over the vast Abrupt,

                                                art,

All circumspection:

The weight of all

                    transcendent

                        silence

                out of
                    this huge convex of fire,

Ninefold

        unknown

in the shape

as of

above the

rose

through

rose

rising

the radiant sun

Extend
The birds their notes

                          though under

            earth,

A globe   enclosed

Toward the four winds four
                          sounding
                                  the hollow
              far and wide, and all

            restless

With rapid wheels,

                in the clouds

                                    of arms
From either end

                    rocks and hills
In whirlwind;

              from the top

              a silent valley, sing

                        the Soul,
                          a hill

                                        absolute—
                                  maze
Of good and evil

                                  triple

Four
Of four
Into the burning
                    flood

Hear

                labyrinth
                              being

beat with perpetual

all else deep snow and ice,

the effect of fire

At certain revolutions

extremes, extremes by change
in ice
to pine

Immovable,

with one small drop

so near the brink;

The lip of

rest.

life dies, death lives,

on swift wings

Now shaves with level wing the deep,
Up

                    toward the pole:
                         At last appear

          thrice threefold

                    with circling fire,
                         the gates
On either side

                    —a serpent armed

                                   womb,

Within unseen.
                    bathing in the sea that parts

                    the air

                    The other Shape—
          it might be called that shape had none

                    : what seemed his head

          now at hand,

                         as he strode.

Through them I mean to pass,

Unbroken

      against the Highest—

          like a comet burned,

In the arctic sky

               at the head

Levelled

             front to front

             mid–air.

"O father,

               O son,

head?

and thy words so strange

double-formed, and

phantasm

Surprised
In darkness,

Out of thy head I sprung.   Amazement seized

                in secret
        growing
And fields

Through all the Empyrean.
            headlong
Into this Deep;
I also: key

Without my opening.

Alone;

        motion felt and

Transformed:

From all her caves,

                  conceived

     with conscious

       eyes in opposition

  me,

           bright arms,

          unthought-of—

From out this dark

To search,
                    by concurring signs,
Created vast and round—

        our vacant room   .

                                    designed
To know;

    "The key

To sit in

My being

                              without end."

then in the key-hole turns
The intricate

Unfastens

Without dimension; where length, breadth,
time, and place, are lost;

Eternal

embryon atoms

as the sands

warring winds, and poise
adhere
a moment:

Chance governs all.

              to
                frame

          in the surging smoke

Instinct with fire

                      half on foot,
Half flying;

With head, hands, wings, or feet,
    swim

        through the hollow

           to meet there whatever

Bordering on light;

               , eldest of things,

                  name

          with a thousand   mouths.

Night,

                                up to light,

Alone

                    Direct my course:

(Which is my present journey)

Yours be the

              speech

I saw and heard

                        far and wide

                like a pyramid of fire,

                  on all sides round

betwixt the

        Whirlpool

   alteration!

Pave

     bridge of
       reach

      from the walls

       resembling air,

Far off
In circuit,

This pendent World,
     close by the moon.

radi os

o III

H^{ail}

Bright effluence of bright essence

Whose fountain

                              at the voice

The rising World

Through
                    the Orphean

        descent, and up

To find
                      the more

Clear
             song;

Nightly I visit:

Blind
        thoughts that voluntary move
Harmonious numbers

                summer's rose,

Shine inward, and
      there plant eyes
           that I may see and tell
Of things invisible

                 once

    thick as stars,

The radiant image

                        the only
                          Garden

On the bare outside of this World,

            no bars of Hell, nor

      far off Heaven,

And Man there placed,

                the sole command,

       create

                    or love

So were created,
        Maker,

                by absolute

                impulse
                immutably foreseen,

                                                change
Unchangeable, eternal

                                        measure
        uttering

                with the innumerable sound
Encompassed

Of all things made,

creation

Be question

                          replied:—

My word, my

                  desires:

Upheld by
      ground

             of peculiar grace,

The rest shall hear

              their senses dark

                      not shut
        within them as

Light after light
   to the end

Against the high

                    naught

                         where shall we find such love?
                    mortal, to redeem

                                        mute

                         Death

In whom

Atonement

Account me Man:

                                   to possess
Life in myself for ever; by

All that of me can die

the ample air

at the sight
shalt look down

the grave;
Then,
enter Heaven, long absent,
to see thy face, wherein no cloud

but

breath

and Earth

Made flesh, when time shall be,

The head of all

transplanted

love shall outdo
death, and dying

                                   assume
Man's nature,

      fruition
      from utter loss, and

      under thee,

    in the sky appear

                    from all winds

      such a peal

The World shall burn

          to compass all

multitude
　　　from numbers without number,
　　　　　uttering

The eternal

　　　　　　　　　　　　　　ground

　　crown

　　　　　Tree of Life,

　　　　　　　　inwreathed with

　　song

　　　　　　　　　of all being,
Fountain of

Dark with excessive bright

　　　　　　　　　　, without cloud

　　　　behold:

                    thunder
     flaming   wheels
              frame

              Man: him, through
    Father

                          matter
                               harp

                                  the Starry Sphere,
                          and hymn

    The luminous
                          inroad of Darkness

                                  from the wall of

         glimmering air
                          at large in

         snowy

              flesh

this windy

aerial

other

Dissolved on Earth,

as some have dreamed:

Translated

crystalline   balance

cross wind

                                    upwhirled aloft,

Into a Limbo

Of dawning light turned

                        thick with sparkling

        stairs

And waking cried, *This*
Each
                    underneath a

Rapt

                        ascent

Direct against

                    the Earth—

All night,

                              aware

With glistering spires and

        wonder seized,

                    the circling
                    extended shade

                              from pole to pole

Through the pure marble air

                         :

The golden Sun,
        his eye.

The Universe,   to each inward part

The place

                              informed
                                    with fire

Imagined

                        from the sea,

          in the dark

                    to gaze
Undazzled.
          sight no obstacle

Shadow from body opaque can fall

To objects

                        also in the Sun.

Man,

His journey's end,

his proper shape,

his radiant visage turned
by   ear

to the Earth

—

his eye
Creation round—
desire to see and know

Alone

Worlds,
That both in him and all things,

              drive
   deepest

                 Sun,

                   are all his works,

        created mind

                    Infinitude confined;

          quintessence

              turned to star

Man; that light
which else,

Still ending, still renewing,

                                        is Paradise,
Adam's

            ecliptic,
                in many an aery wheel

radi os

O IV

O for
 The Apocalypse

                              that now,
While time was, our
    coming of

                    flame

To
                              flight

                                   the birth

from the bottom stir

One step

wakes
what is,

and the full-blazing
meridian
revolving

in a moment

                              from within

without

                                     to stand

                 equally to all

Among the Spirit

By act of grace,

                           and void

            : so should I

    know

Divided

                              eye beheld:
          clear
Artificer of

                         whose eye pursued him down

          steep

                                   shade,
                           and branching
Shade above shade,

                                   up–sprung
Into
                    that

On which the sun

                         of pure now
                                   drive
All

Blest,

the ascent of

one continued

beast that
looked
On the other side

sheer
Light

amid the field

Of
Cross-barred
fold:
into
the Tree of

them who lived;

Of immortality.

Beneath
        of human sense exposed,

    the garden
          stretched

Of vegetable gold; and next to life,
Our death,

                  raised
            through veins
Of porous earth
Rose   fountain,

    divided into four main streams,

Rolling

      the morning sun
The open field, and
                place,

      with golden rind

  interposed

                                                            rose

Her crystal mirror holds,

Knit with the

            gathered—
                        through the world—

                                                        eye;

            head, enclosed with shining rock,

The image   Maker

                and
                parted
                        beneath
        as a veil down to

                                        wave
        the vine curl

                                        sway,

        those mysterious

        works

                                        of seeming

    hand in hand

                                on a green
                                    fountain
Of

                        thirst and

                            the brimming stream;

    About

                                              wreath
                    close
              wove with

        line
                              in the ascending scale

                        gaze
              at length

Into our room of
Creatures

                    —whom my thoughts

              that formed them

        vanish

As now is entered;

                              widest gate
              forth
                    narrow limits,

                    World—

                              shape

          By word or
            lion

                                        at play,

              in each paw:
                                  moving speech

                    from the dust, and place

                              —

          So near grows Death to Life,

          Among so many signs

          Unlimited of manifold

                         replied:—"O
And
And
And
For
And
So

That
I

And what I was

            issued from a cave, and spread
Into a liquid plain;

                    to look into the clear

                        opposite

                    .   I started back,
    It started back;

  .

                              'What thou seest,
                                is thyself;

And I will bring thee

        image

Under

                watery image.

Seized

                                       with eyes

           under the flow
                 in

flow

Imparadised in one another's

                            thrust,

Still unfulfilled, with

                All

The proof

                   invented with design
                          exalt

           no corner leave
        but chance

I return,

                              turned,

Through wood,
            in utmost longitude,
                              the setting Sun

Levelled
                        to the clouds,
                              with one ascent
Accessible from

                                    to climb
Betwixt the

                  with diamond flaming
                        gliding through the even

                              compass

                        watch

Bent all on speed,
                        that lies from

            eye pursued

                              the Deep, to raise

                  winged
                        perfect sight,
Amid the Sun's bright circle
See

  meridian

        minded,

                        with corporeal bar.
                within the circuit of
        whatsoever shape,
                                        I shall know."

                on that bright beam,

Diurnal

                                        nightingale.
                                                sung:
        Silence

                                        the Moon,
                                at length

Our eye-lid

                                body

While

                        morning

        walk at noon,

More hands than
        blossom

Ask

                        : to know

                    all time,
All seasons, and their change;

                        the Sun,

    orient
        with dew;

                        or rising

Glistering

        total Dark

In nature and all things

                        shed down
    stellar

                        deep

when we wake,

                        from the steep
            have we heard

harmonic number joined,

                                    The roof
            inwoven

Iris all hues,

Mosaic; under foot the
Crocus,

                worm,

            choir

                        authentic fire.

    and under open sky

And starry Pole:—
    Omni

                crown

                        to the ground.

        when we seek, as now

                disguise

                        refused:

                Love, mysterious law,

                            else!

        bestial

Perpetual fountain of

        past, as

                        mask,

And on

                    and know to know no
                                    shadow   cone
Half-way up-hill this

        issuing

                                power
                                            the south
                                            the north:
Our circuit

                bent (who could have thought?)

                                to
                                            forge
    Illusion

                        from pure blood
                from

            intent

                                    spark

blaze

in wait,

"Know
"Know

The lowest
            and
                    to end as
                            answering
                                    shape the
        undiminished

Departed
            place

                whose charge is

                    added grace

And

        lustre

                —the sender, not the sent;

        "Thy fear,"

                        To strive or fly
        held
        heart,
                            half-rounding

Just met, and, closing,

    "O

                now
          through the shade;

      to part

        what form and

                bounds prescribed

To question
              sleep, and
          planted

        doubt.
                  from Hell,

        to whatever place

            in this place I sought:
      reason

          intends our stay
In that dark durance.
The rest is

    loss

by flying

                              pain

in flight from pain
                    of flight,

            words

                    hazard all

                Abyss, and
        World,

                        mid Air;
    possession put to

                song

    , fit body to fit head!

whence
limits

                                    wheel

Turned fiery
    phalanx,
                        as when a field
                    waving bends

Sway

            Atlas, unremoved:

                the Elements

In counterpoise,   events

For proof look up,

And read
Where thou art

Art is man's teacher, but art is art's teacher. A poet usually finds his poetry in another poet. This process used to be called emulation, was admired and encouraged, but tumbled into disrepute from the Romantics to our day, when the red banner of Originality was carried to the barricades where it still stands. And, inevitably, it was long ago discovered that emulation is one of the most revolutionary forms of originality. The word *invention*, which once meant *finding* rather than making from scratch, now means *finding* again. Look at Eliot, Ives, Pound, Joyce, Picasso, Stravinsky. (The most original writer of our time, Gertrude Stein, still begins *The Making of Americans* with a passage from the Nichomachaean Ethics, and conceals the word *eros* in "A rose is a rose is a rose.")

Ronald Johnson's finding his poem *Radi os* inside *Paradise Lost* is startlingly modern and thoroughly traditional. Insofar as he is making a version of the epic he is in the good company of Wordsworth, Blake, and the Joyce of the *Wake*. And of Milton himself, for to the craftsman's eye, Milton found his poem in the Bible, in Homer, in Virgil, in Joshuah Sylvester's translation of Guillaume de Salluste du Bartas's *La Semaine*, called *Divine Weekes and Workes*, and (as Milton scholars tend not to know) in Serafino della Salandra's *Adamo Caduto*. It would be as accurate to say that Milton found his epic in that fierce spirit of the Baroque that had begun all over Europe to state the tension between exuberance and restraint, between form and content, between the two winds of thought that made the weather of Milton's mind, Greece and Israel. The attempt to harness them both to one tumultuous chariot gave us Racine and Michelangelo, Dürer and Montaigne.

Nor is this the first poem to be precipitated from *Paradise Lost*. *The Prelude* is another, with its translation of the theme into the psychology of Romanticism and its transmutation of the Miltonic phrase to its own ends, whereby Wordsworth can begin his poem with Satan's words appropriated and set in a new context:

> escaped
> From the vast city, where I long had pined
> A discontented soujourner: now free,
> Free as a bird to settle where I will.
> What dwelling shall receive me?

Whether Wordsworth wanted us to hear Satan's voice inside his own here (and identify London with Jerusalem on high, and see Satan's wings in that bird, and hear the anguish of the outcast in the question) is the same consideration Ronald Johnson invites throughout his text. At least two voices are speaking: Milton's and Ronald Johnson's.

Blake also rewrote *Paradise Lost*, once as the unfinished epic called *Vala* or *A Dream of Nine Nights* or *The Book of Moonlight*, and once as his poem *Milton*. Blake was correcting and amplifying Milton; he was *opening him up*, as he said. Some day someone will explain why the Romantics wanted to rewrite *Paradise Lost* and the moderns to rewrite the *Odyssey*. And then we will have a clearer understanding of why Ronald Johnson returned, as a signal act of the postmodernist period (The Age of Olson the books will get around to naming it), to Milton. Part of the answer will be that Ronald Johnson began as a latter-day disciple of Blake.

His first poems are modelled on the visionary concerns of a group of young men who used to visit Blake in his old age.

It was an October afternoon in 1824—the year of Byron's death, Beethoven's Ninth, and the completion of the Erie Canal—that the portraitist John Linnell took the young Samuel Palmer to meet William Blake. (If you translate Palmer into a poet, you have Ronald Johnson, not exactly, but close enough.) They found him working in bed on the illustrations to Dante which Linnell had commissioned. (He also commissioned the Job engravings.)

For Palmer, a Baptist and an artist, his mind shaped by scripture, Bunyan, and Milton, it was one of those radiant encounters in which a disciple found his master. Blake had but three years to live. He was old, troubled by piles and gallstones, but his mind was as bright and as fertile as ever. In another, more prosperous, part of London Charles Babbage was building the grandfather of all computers. The steam locomotive had been invented and was already wobbling along a few short rails. The world said that it was now rational, scientific, progressive. When Palmer stepped into Blake's simple house at Fountain Court it was as if he had erased three thousand years of history and stepped into the tent of Isaiah.

Palmer, in turn, brought his mystical friend the pagan painter and engraver Edward Calvert, and eventually an enclave of enthusiastic young men who began to call themselves The Ancients —Palmer's cousin John Giles, the Rev. Arthur Tatham and his brother Frederick, the painter George Richmond, Francis Oliver Finch, Henry Walker, and Welby Sherman. Only Calvert and Palmer survive in history; Linnell is half-remembered; the others deserve to have their names kept in the list, epic-fashion, because they brightened the last days of Blake and because they are the first members of a family that exists to this day.

Ronald Johnson is very much an Ancient of the tribe of William. The world into which he came (out of Kansas) offered encounters with Charles Olson and Louis Zukofsky, who both had been friends of Ezra Pound, channel of traditions (from him you could be one remove from James, Yeats, Ford, Joyce, or if you were so minded, Brancusi, Gaudier-Brzeska, Cocteau, Gourmont, or again, Wyndham Lewis, Eliot, H.D., John Quinn). At this writing Zukofsky, our greatest living poet, is not considered to be our greatest living poet; Olson is slowly being read and studied. Our liveliest literary tradition, as usual, is an unknown, even an unsuspected one. It is Ronald

Johnson's tradition, his family, and the custodian of the things he honors. He came to it through his Iolian friend of a decade, Jonathan Williams, lyrical and satiric master of rhythms and images, whose masters are Olson, Zukofsky, Catullus, Bunting, and the great god Apollo himself.

Ronald Johnson's fund of imagery and tones goes back to Ruskin's precision in description and Thoreau's exact knowledge of nature, back to the visionary eyes of Palmer, Dove, and Burchfield. All that is particular in its splendor belongs to his imagination, Audubon and John Ireland, Cheval the French postman who built an Ideal Palace out of rocks picked up for twenty years, Satie, Arnold Bax, Victorian diarists. He once described my lawn in Kentucky as "all Klimt with violets."

From book to book he has grown more responsive to light and pattern in nature; he believes that light evolved the eye to see itself, an idea that would have made a stir among the Platonists at Chartres in the twelfth century, or in the study of Bishop Grosseteste at Lincoln. The major books are *A Line of Poetry, A Row of Trees* (1963), *The Different Musics* (1967)—both collected in *Valley of the Many-Colored Grasses* (1969)—*The Book of the Green Man* (1967), *Songs of the Earth* (1970), and the great work now in the writing, *Ark*, part one of which is finished, part four of which may be *Radi os*.

The paradox of originality houses many rooms, and the views from the windows are all different. What the artist seems to create has, as the artist is the first to appreciate and acknowledge, already been created. Design and arrangement are the artist's passion. *Place* is all. The painters of Lascaux found their horses in the rock. Wherever there was a bulge in the cave wall that suggested equine solidity, they surrounded it with an elegance of mane, legs, and tail. The nose was drawn first, then, in a masterful stroke, the beautiful line from face to butt, the horizon of horse. We have found this line all by itself, whether unfinished or sufficient to say "horse" we shall never know. This line survives in the Chinese ideogram meaning horse, *ma*, together with the prancing legs that are man's first graph of the verb *to move*. Poetry and painting have a passport through time; historical cycles which are the essence of a work of art to the historian are the artist's last consideration. So there is no anomaly in Ronald Johnson's choosing Milton to fuse into a new poetic symbiosis. The choice, however, was pure genius.

Toward the end of the nineteenth century Milton was already going out of fashion. Men with the surest command of English—especially the two masters Doughty and Hopkins—were turning away from the Renaissance donation of English diction and going back to native words and phrases. Yeats and Pound (outlanders, note) completed the process toward a natural, genial diction, and Milton was damned for writing no English at all. He was artificial. He was Latinate. (This is illusion. Eighty per cent of the words in *Paradise Lost* are of Anglo-Saxon derivation. Milton used far fewer Latinisms than Gibbon, and only sixty per cent of Shakespeare's words are of English origin. And he was the most sparing of stylists—the word *afternoon* occurs but once in all his writing, *abrupt*, *inconvenient*, and *American*.)

Milton was indeed artificial. His sonorous, highly pictorial style was evolved to impose classical form on one of the most energetic languages since Greek. A meticulously conscious artist in an age that knew the usefulness of art, Milton understood exactly where he was in history, and what he had to do to give his art its step in the pace of time.

Time, Pythagoras had said, is the mind of the stars. The book in which you could have found that sentence was printed in Paris in 1552, a translation into Latin of Plutarch's *On the Generation of the Soul*. Within the decade men would be born in England who would invent a poetry which they imagined was like that of the ancient world. All Europe by this time knew that a lost world was being recovered, a world that contained Plato and Homer, Pythagoras and Plutarch, Diodorus the Sicilian, St. Jerome and Virgil, Ovid and Catullus.

The first bright dawn of the Renaissance in England did not take time to study the economy of tone of the Greek and Latin which it was eager to have in English. With the old genius of British poetry the first translators went at their matter undaunted, godlike. Here is Arthur Golding doing Ovid:

> She scarce had said these words, but that she leaped on the wave,
> And getting to the ships by force of strength that Love hir gave,
> Upon the King of *Candies* Keele in spight of him she clave.
> Whome when hir father spide (for now he hovered in the aire,
> And being made a Hobby Hauke did soare between a paire
> Of nimble wings on yron Mayle) he soused down a maine
> To seaze upon hir as she hung, and would have torn hir faine
> With bowing Beake.

George Chapman translating Homer:

> This shield thus done, he forg'd for him such curets as outshin'd
> The blaze of fire. A helmet then (through which no steele could find
> Forc't passage) he composde, whose hue a hundred colours tooke;
> And in the crest a plume of gold, that each breath stirr'd, he stucke.
> All done, he all to Thetis brought, and held up all to her.
> She took them all, and like t' the hawke (surnamed the Osspringer),
> From Vulcan to her mightie sonne, with that so glorious show,
> Stoopt from the steepe Olympian hill, hid in eternall snow.

This robustness and headlong meter would be tamed by Marlowe, Shakespeare, Jonson, Spenser, each in his own tone (Shakespeare in a hundred tones), yet the energy remained, and the idiom remained English, glorious English. In this second perfection of the language (the first was Chaucer), the Bible was translated with a majesty of phrasing, a music of nuance and pause, a strength of diction that has never been equalled in any version of scripture:

> Lift up your heads, O yee gates,
> And be ye lift up ye everlasting doores;
> And the King of glory shall come in.
> Who is this king of glory?
> The LORD strong and mightie,
> The LORD mighty in battell.

The poet who would achieve a new vision of English poetry and turn it irrevocably toward the pure models of Greek and Latin was the latecomer Milton. As a baby he could have looked out the window and seen Shakespeare and Jonson in their tall, dove-gray felt hats and royal blue capes, for he lived on the street that one took to get to the tavern with a mermaid on its shingle.

We have no notion what served Shakespeare for religion, the scholarly and stubborn Jonson was sometimes Protestant, sometimes Catholic; English intellectuals were apt to run to Corinthian manners until reminded by the cannon's mouth or the headsman's ax that they were Christians. The young Milton was pious and grave, a Puritan with something of a private theology (as his greatest emulator Blake knew very well). Like other Puritans he was a humanist, cherishing pagan lore for its beauty and wisdom (Cotton Mather read his Ovid along with his Calvin). He dyed his mind with Latin, Greek, and Hebrew at Cambridge, did the grand tour (Galileo let him look through his telescope, and probably assured him in whispers that Copernicus was right: the earth is a planet among others that circles the sun, which great light, like God, moves all without itself moving).

He became Latin secretary to Protector Cromwell (on whose guns was inscribed "God is Love"), and here he read and wrote himself blind. When the king returned, he withdrew into a houseful of daughters and composed his epic. We are told that he got the lines straight in his head upon waking, and in the freshness of the morning announced that he was ready to be milked. He sat across a chair, his back against one arm, his knees over the other. One visitor described him in a suit of rusty green, and we are told that before bedtime he regaled himself with the pleasure of a pipe of Virginia tobacco and a cold glass of water. Even in his blindness he wore his sword.

The great poem he dictated—twice, as he expanded it almost immediately after its first edition from ten to twelve books—was the greatest verbal expression of the Baroque style which culminates the Renaissance, aggrandizing its spirit to a lyric grandeur. Music to Shakespeare was the lute; to Milton, the organ.

While he dictated, the long rule of Louis XIV began, no rain fell in India for three whole years, Velazquez painted the Spanish court and Vermeer Dutch housewives pouring milk, the Turks cut their way through Hungary and Transylvania toward Vienna, and certain children were born and baptized Daniel Defoe, Henry Purcell, Matthew Prior. In the American colonies Michael Wigglesworth published *The Day of Doom*, which sold more copies than any book of poetry ever published in this country.

And three hundred and ten years later a poet in San Francisco sits down with the text and begins to erase it. So that it now begins: "O tree into the World, Man the chosen Rose out of Chaos: song." Trees come into the world (from seeds underground) in answer to light, and once there they convert our breath into oxygen which we breathe again, and they digest light in order to ferment water and minerals which they have brought up from the earth into a nourishing green, which we can eat, or eat the animal that has eaten the green. No tree, no man. We rose out of chaos together, and the rose is an order of petals symbolizing the opposite of chaos.

The poem we are reading is still Milton's, but sifted. The spare scattering of words left on the page continues to make a coherent poem, Milton *imagiste*. (Wordsworth and Blake did the same thing to the poem, except that they filled up the spaces again with their own words.) Strange and wonderful things happen on these pages. Here, for instance, Milton is made to anticipate the first Duino Elegy:

<pre>
            Who, from the terror of this
                    empyreal
            Irreconcilable
                                        of joy
                    answered
            Too well I see
                    : for the mind
</pre>

                swallowed up

                                                entire,

        in the heart   to work in fire,

                        words the Arch

   These pages at first glance look haphazard (as a Cubist painting
seemed to first viewers to be an accident). They are not. There is a
page that has the word *man* at the top, *flower* in the middle, and *star*
at the bottom. There are other words on the page, and they help us
see the relationship between man, flower, and star. One order of
words gives: "man passed through fire / His temple right against the
black." It is, for instance, electrochemical energy in brain cells de-
rived from photosynthetic sugars in vegetables whereby we can see
a star at all, and the fire of the star we call the sun thus arranged that
it could be seen and thought of by nourishing the brain. Is that sys-
tem closed? Did the sun grow the tree that made the paper you are
holding, and the ink on it, so that it can read this book through your
eyes?
   The eye as a kind of scanner for the sun is an idea with a glimpse
of God in it. It is knowledge. In Milton's myth man was created to
be like a lion, with instincts. Such a creature fulfills itself by being
an excellent lion (the rose knows nothing but to be a rose). He feels,
breeds, fights, eats, sleeps. He will never know the harmony of
numbers or compose a partita. He will never build an Ideal Palace
or tell a folktale to his nieces or nephews. But he lives in a paradise.
If he were to lose that paradise, he would have to begin finding it
again.
   He would know he was in an alien state, and his knowledge
would be tragic. The knowledge of good and evil that man chose
turned out to be (as he could not have suspected) meaningless. He
could know facts, which are neutral, heartless, apt to serve one
opinion as well as another. To knowledge must be added grace. It
is at this turning of Milton's plot that Ronald Johnson seems to have
become interested in following Milton through his maze of words,

intent on mining a particular ore, on isolating, for greater clarity, a single radiant quality.

When Satan (who is the essence of nothing) tempted man into knowledge, he exiled him from lionhood, from a harmony with creation. We can call this a blindness, and the search for understanding a hunger for vision. It was Blake who saw that seeing eyes can be perfectly blind, that they can see without that special gift of apprehension that he identified with Christ, redemption, and grace. Milton calls the mind "infinitude confined" (Ronald Johnson retains these words in his erasure).

Nature has no nothing. To feel that it has is what we call the devil, the enemy. In Blakean words, our predicament is that we can exist and still not be, for being requires an awakeness from the dream of custom and of ourselves. The self is by nature turned outward to connect with the harmony of things. The eyes cannot see themselves, but something other. The strange and paradoxical rule of nature is that we are fullest in our being by forgetting our being. To love nothing is to be nothing, to give is to have.

Radii are the lines outward from a center. We exist because of the radii of the sun (because of the radii of God, Milton would say). Radiance, wheel after wheel of it, whether or benevolence or music or attention, is a basic pattern of life.

Knowledge is a kind of ignorance, ignorance a kind of knowledge. This peculiarly American perception runs through our literature, welling up from our experience. Wind brought us over, pushing sails, and spirit brought us over, pushing minds, and our greatest efforts have always been to harness energy. With forgivable innocence and unforgivable arrogance we mistook the knowledge of others for ignorance as often as we mistook our ignorance for knowledge. Learning has always therefore been a conversion for us. Our literature is one of persuasion and discovery, of vision.

Behind the mask of custom there is a natural life, our poets have always said; inside history, light. Our calipers for taking the measure of nature have never been on a human scale. Melville saw that a spermatozoon is a microscopic whale. Gertrude Stein, remembering Emerson, said that moonlight in a valley is before and after history. Poe could find a symbol for all of European civilization—Alaric the Visigoth's black crow surmounting a bust of Athene—and make a ghost story of it. We have sought a thoroughly enigmatic and inclusive symbol of the world in all our art, showing fear in a handful of dust, affection in a handful of grass ("I guess it is the handkerchief of the Lord"), death in the buzz of a fly.

Foragers by destiny, we like to go into familiar places and make a new report of the contents—Henry Adams to Chartres, Pound to China, Olson to the Yucatán. All too characteristically we have no notion what we're looking for; we are simply looking. Something, we feel—the national hunch—is always there. Louis Zukofsky began writing *"A"* in 1925, finishing it fifty years later (the first long American poem to be finished since Melville's *Clarel*), making it up as he went along, like an architect who put in a foundation without any idea whether he would continue in glass or brick. So Olson wrote his *Maximus*, Williams his *Paterson*, Pound his *Cantos*, Whitman his *Leaves of Grass*.

Ronald Johnson is writing a long poem called *Ark*, various schema on his worktable, visions in his head. It is a poem that grows naturally out of the concerns of his earlier poetry, unfolding them like a sunrise maturing toward noontide. But no sooner had he moved into this complex and brilliant poem, a masterpiece of new forms and rhythms, than he (true American forager) found an idea along the way. He found a poem inside another poem. All he had to do was to remove the superfluous words.

Works of art in response to other works of art create a symbolic chord reaching across the two. Ulysses in Ithaca, Ulysses in Dublin: a web of meaning not entirely under Joyce's control bridges the extremes and begins generating ratios. We can recognize in Ronald Johnson's derived poem an image of America as a paradise lost; it is a theme of the times. We can recognize the constant American theme of wondering all over again what to do with the gift of creation. Milton had the sense that the Reformation was waking the human spirit to things it had abandoned through error and negligence. It is a valid and perhaps urgent purpose for poetry to speak to a people who, at worst, have no vision of the gift of being other than to make money, slide (or rip) around in an automobile, and to spend the rest of their time before a box that alternately informs them that Haley's M.O. unclogs the sluggish bowel and that fighting continues in the streets of Beirut.

Radi os is a meditation, first of all, on grace. It finds in Milton's poems those clusters of words which were originally a molecular intuition of the complex harmony of nature whereby eyesight loops back to its source in the sun, the earth, the tree, our cousin animals, the spiralling galaxies, and mysteriously to the inhuman black of empty space. Out of these elements ("creation" was Milton's word) arose our imagined gods and our social order. At the center of the Greek spirit was a meditation on the origin of wheat. (By analogy the center of the American spirit should be a temple to petroleum, but we don't have even that.)

As I write this a spaceship is circling Mars, its computer eyes looking for a place to land. It will report back, if it functions, that there is nothing there but desolation. A similar voyage to all the other planets will report nothing, nothing, nothing. That we are alone in a universe of red stars and white stars, a catastrophe of light and electric thunder of time, vibrant forever, forever bright, fifty-eight sextillion, seven hundred quintillion, seven hundred and sixty quadrillion miles wide (by Einstein's reckoning), is the plain fact our age will have to learn to live with, as Milton in his lifetime had to learn that the earth is a planet of the sun, a smallish star.

The astronomers are beginning to tell us about events in space called black holes and naked particularities. Some cycle has made a revolution and come around again to a point where Milton made a vision of the world and of man's place in it. That our new moment is still somehow Miltonic is Ronald Johnson's discovery, a discovery that only a poet could make, a discovery that enhances and sharpens our sense of poetry and opens our eyes in a new way to the world.

Guy Davenport

LEXINGTON, 1976 / 1981

A NOTE ON THE TEXT

Radi os was originally published in 1977 by Sand Dollar Books in Berkeley, California. The plates for that edition were created in facsimile from *The Poetical Works of John Milton* (New York: Thomas Y. Crowell & Company, 1892). The present edition has been redesigned and digitally typeset by Jeff Clark of Quemadura, retaining the orthography and spacing of the original.